The Harvest Craft Book

Thomas Berger

The Harvest Craft Book

Floris Books

Translated by Polly Lawson
Photographs by Wim Steenkamp and Thomas Berger
Illustrations by Ronald Heuninck

First published in Dutch under the title *Herfstversieringen*
by Christofoor Publishers in 1992
First published in English in 1992 by Floris Books
Reprinted in 1993

British Library CIP Data available

ISBN 0-86315-147-7

Printed in the Netherlands

Contents

Foreword

At no other season of the year is nature so generous with her gifts as in the autumn. After a period of growth and blossoming in spring and in summer, flowers and leaves, seeds and fruit simply lie there ready as it were to be picked up.

With their wealth of form and colour they are particularly suitable for making innumerable decorations and little models which can find their place in front of the window, on the wall or on a little table reserved for the season's decorations.

In this book I wish to show what endless possibilities there are for making decorations with all the gifts of nature which otherwise we might pass unheedingly.

For many years now our family has collected chestnuts, acorns, beech-nuts, autumn leaves and so on, from which we have made all sorts of things. In this way gradually one acquires a better eye for the incredible beauty of nature. For example just look at the various kinds of grain with their great wealth of form and colour brought about partly by the place where they grow, the nature of the soil and the climate.

Of all the cereals, corn (maize) is the plant which provides the finest material with which to work: the magnificent tassels (panicles) above the stalk; the leaf-sheaths of the cob, which when dried are most suitable for making dolls (see Figure 48) or cut into strips for plaiting mats; the "silks" (stigma-threads) which when wetted can be braided into hair-plaits (see Figure 51) and the grains themselves which can be threaded together to make autumn garlands (see Figure 72).

Little discoveries can give us an inspiration: once when we were looking at a pine-cone the tiny filmy seeds fell out from among the scales as they opened out in the warmth. The way in which the seeds floated down to the ground gave us the idea of using them to make a winged creature, and in this way the little bee of Figure 64 came into being.

Autumn is primarily the harvest time, but when we look into nature we find that a great deal of the harvest has already begun in the summer. Depending on the warmth of the sun, grain for example is ready for harvesting in July or August. So do not wait until the autumn gales burst upon us at the end of September, but start collecting your materials and drying them out already during the summer. Remember to take a bag with you on your walks for any chance finds.

In the course of the year's festivals there are three which belong in the autumn: September 29 is Michaelmas, the feast of Michael and his angels, October 31 is Hallowe'en, and on November 11, Martinmas, the festival of St Martin is celebrated especially with children on the continent of Europe.

Ancient accounts and legends tell how the Archangel Michael was appointed by God the Father in heaven to undertake the battle with the adversary Lucifer, who was then overthrown and cast upon the earth as a devil or dragon. That is why Michael is so often depicted as the victor over the dragon. But there are also pictures which show him as the weigher of souls, as the one who stands at the gate of heaven weighing the harvest of a human life.

Hallowe'en has its origin in the Celtic festival of Samhain, which celebrated the first day of winter on November 1. The spirits of the dead and other supernatural creatures — fairies, witches and goblins — were about on that night. The light of fires and lanterns warded off the evil spirits. Turnip and pumpkin lanterns are like the last afterthought of the summer's ripening strength.

St Martin, according to the legends, lived in the fourth century. He was a soldier who gave half of his cloak to a poor beggar. Then in a dream St Martin saw a Figure of light who told him that he had given his cloak to Christ.

The last chapter of this book describes a number of things (including the dragon) for a Michaelmas festival, as well as lanterns for Hallowe'en.

It is not our intention that you should just copy the models in this book. They are made and described simply to stimulate you in the hope that you will go further with your own ideas and variations.

For most of the autumn decorations in this book the necessary materials are simply lying in natural surroundings ready to be picked up, so you do not need to break off things from woods, garden or park.

1 Decorating and Assembling

In this chapter there are a few general tips on decorating and setting up, for example, a wreath, a pine-cone or one of the plaits described in the next chapter. These require quite simple techniques using all kinds of things which are to be found in the garden, park, grass-verges or woods. For example:

Cereals and grasses
The leaf-sheaths of the maize-cob
The silks (hairlike stigma) of the corn cob
The tassels (panicles) of corn (maize)
Pine-cones (even the remains gnawed by
    squirrels)
Larch-cones
Alder-cones
Conifer-cones
Acorns
Beech-nuts
Hop-cones
Hogweed-blossom
Honesty-pennies
Dried leaves
Hydrangea flowers
Maple seeds
All these materials must of course be thoroughly dried.

Drying the flowers

During the whole year all sorts of flowers such as roses, thistles, gypsophila (chickweed, maiden's breath) and so on, can be dried by hanging them up by their stalks in a dark dry place. It is best not to leave the flowers in a vase until they are just about finished, but to hang them up well before they wilt.

Mounting harvest materials on wire

Materials
Various harvest findings
Thin wire ($1/8''$–$3/16''$, 0.4 mm)
Wire-clippers

Method
To make a corsage, bouquet or posy we use fine wire to bind together each separate item. Thus grasses, beech-nuts, and so on, can be firmly bound together to make an artistic whole. As can be seen in Figure 1 we keep the stems as short as possible, otherwise with too many stems the posy becomes too thick. The wire holds the stems together.

There are various methods:

1 Fixing wire to a stalk

Take a piece of wire about 6" (15 cm) long, bend it double making a loop with one end pointing down (see Figure 1a-c). Now take a wheat stalk, for example, and hold it tight between your thumb and forefinger so that the loop can be passed round it. Let one end of the wire lie against the stalk and wind the other end three or four times tightly round them and then let then ends of the wire lie next to each other. Of course it is also possible to set several stalks together on to wire in this way. Make sure that the two loose ends of the wire are of about the same length, so that when the posy is finished they will give it enough support.

2 Fixing wire to leaves or honesty-pennies

For this again we need a piece of fine wire about 6" (15 cm) long. Push one end of the wire through the leaf a little bit above the lower edge and bend it carefully downwards (Figure 1d, 1e). Take the leaf between your thumb and forefinger and wind one end of the wire two or three times tightly round the other end and then bring it straight down.

3 Fixing wire to pine-cones and such like

As the cones dry the scales open. This enables a wire to be passed through the bottom row of scales near the stalk (Figure 1f, 1g). Again twist one end of the wire a few times round the other.

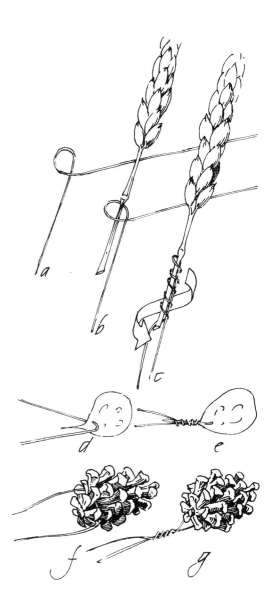

Figure 1.

Figure 2.

Making a posy

Materials
Various harvest findings
Thin wire (¹/₈″–³/₁₆″, 0.4 mm)
Wire-clippers

Materials
Various harvest findings
Thin wire (¹/₈″–³/₁₆″, 0.4 mm)
Wire-clippers

Method
Figure 4 shows the various stages in making a posy.

First choose the materials which you wish to use for the posy and set them on wire (see page 10).

Begin with a long object such as an ear of corn. Then choose something to go with it and hold both articles in one hand while with the other twist the wires of each article once round

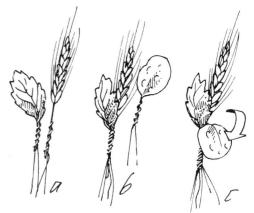

Figure 4.

Figure 3.

each other so that they are firmly attached, but do not go on twisting the wire otherwise you will get an unnecessarily thick lump in the posy. Now take a leaf or a sprig of conifer, for example, and lay it over the wire of the first two materials. Now twist the wire round this once, and the wire of the first two materials will no longer be visible.

In this way one thing after the other can be added. Look carefully at the posy from the front so as to see where the next piece is to come, attach it firmly there and do not pull things which are already attached round to one side, for then the whole posy may come adrift.

To conceal the wire-stems attach one or more leaves to the posy and then bend them back over the wire (see Figure 4). In this way an opening can come about in the "heart" of the posy and this can be filled with something round such as a pine-cone, or a sprig of conifer.

Once the posy is finished you can take a piece of wire out of the middle and twist this firmly round the other wires, cutting off the end at the required length with your wire-clippers.

Tie up the posy firmly with a piece of wire — or with needle and thread — round a plaited wreath, a little piece of wood (see Figure 3) or something similar.

the materials have to be stuck into the lump of clay the ends of the wire should not be too long.

If it is difficult to insert the materials prick some holes in the plastic beforehand with a large needle.

The decorated cone can be hung up or laid down.

Decorating a pine-cone

Materials
A large pine-cone
A lump of modelling clay, diameter about 1″
	(2.5 cm)
A piece of thin plastic (as from a plastic bag)
A piece of ribbon
A piece of wire (thickness about $1/32$″, 0.7 mm)
Various autumn materials set on wire

Method
For decorating a pine-cone it is preferable to use materials from a wood. Once the pine-cone is thoroughly dry and the scales open, pass a piece of wire round through the scales near the stem. Place the lump of clay in a little piece of plastic (which helps to keep it firm) and attach it firmly to the pine-cone by the wire together with a bow of ribbon. The lump of clay will thus come to sit more or less between the scales. Cut off the wire ends as short as possible, even bending back the sharp ends and sticking them into the lump of clay. The pine-cone can now be hung up, and it is best to make it up hanging with the materials already set on wire. Because

Figure 5.

Decorating a wreath

Materials
A wreath of oasis (florist's flower block)
Various autumn materials set on wire

Method
The round wreath symbolizes eternity; there is no beginning and no end. Try to incorporate this element as you add things, so that neither beginning nor end is apparent. Insert all the materials in the same direction, overlapping, thus making a bandage round the wreath (Figure 7). Insert the materials towards you into the oasis. Lay each fresh ear of corn or cone over the last so that the bandage round the wreath grows larger and larger.

Figure 6.

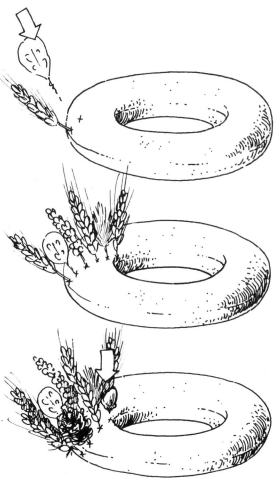

Figure 7.

2 Working with Straw

From the time when grain became food for Humankind, after the harvest had been gathered in, the harvesters would make from the last sheaf of corn a harvest symbol which was then offered to the gods as thanksgiving for an abundant harvest and as a prayer for a new fruitful year. Thus for example in ancient Egypt the straw was made into a doll, the *grain-mother*.

Through the centuries the form of this grain-mother or straw-doll changed, and so with the coming of Christianity there came the harvest-cross, which at the end of the harvest was borne to the church (see Figure 21).

Right up to the beginning of this century many plaited symbols were made in England (and also in other places in Europe); among them there are those known as "corn-dollies."

With combine-harvesters, which thresh the corn and bale the straw at the same time, the custom of making a doll from the last sheaf has lapsed, and with it the skill of plaiting straw has also vanished. Some straw decorations described here are based on traditional motifs, others are new designs.

Tools required

A pair of garden clippers or old scissors (straw is really hard and scissors soon become blunt)

A pair of scissors with sharp points (for finishing off)

A kitchen knife (for removing thin leaves from the stem)

Thin string or stout thread (button-thread) in natural colours

Thick needles

A tape-measure

Straw decorations

For making autumn decorations from straw and ears of corn it is best to use wheat or rye ears (see Figure 8). Wheat-straw is generally the easiest to use as it is fairly pliant.

Depending on the weather, harvesting takes place in July or August. To obtain straw or whole ears ask a farmer just before the corn is cut. See that the corn is not too near a highway, for the grain can be rather grey and dirty.

Sometimes you can find some ears still standing along the edge of the corn-field after the cutting, or the harvester has left some cut corn which has not been threshed. For convenience this will be called "waste straw." Wind and rain will often rob it of its golden-yellow lustre leaving it a greenish colour. Even though

15

the stalks are often broken and flattened they are still quite usable. The models of Figures 13, 14 and 17 are made of this waste straw. Finally of course you can grow your own corn in a sunny patch of your garden.

When working with straw we do not always need stalks *with* ears, which can be cut off at the first nodule. If, however, the *whole stalk* is required see that the ear stands up nicely.

When the *whole stalk* is used in plaiting, then the straw of wheat, and especially the ear with the chaff-husks, is the best as it has a beautiful form. Also the barley-ear with grains in two rows makes a splendid decorative effect. The light, airy oat is generally used only for decoration.

The colour of the ears is partly determined by the composition of the soil on which it grows. Soil containing iron can give a reddish-brown ear, as may be seen on the wheat with chaff-husks in Figure 8.

The Stalks

The stalk consists of a long stem with nodules at regular intervals. Out of these nodules grow long narrow leaves which are wrapped round the stalk. The stalk is thicker at the bottom than up at the ear — becoming thinner at each nodule.

The further apart the nodules the better the stalk is suited for plaiting, for the nodules are tough and cannot be bent easily. If the stalks are very thick at the bottom and very thin at the top then it is best to use only the middle part of the stalk, for the lower part is then often too hard to plait, and the top looks too thin.

The straws are best stored by binding them together with an elastic band and hanging the bunch upside down (reducing the chance of breaking the ears).

The length of the straws depends on the type of grain, where it grows, the humidity and the temperature in the springtime. The length to be used will be determined by the kind of work to be done.

Figure 8. Various kinds of cereal. From left to right: wheat with chaff-husks, wheat, rye, oats, barley-ears with grains in six rows, barley-ears with grains in two rows.

A bouquet of various cereals

Materials
A basket
Oasis (florist's flower block)
A knife
Various kinds of cereals: oat, wheat, rye and
   barley

Method
Cut out a good piece of the oasis measured so
that it fits neatly into the basket, leaving about
$\frac{3}{4}''$ (1.5–2 cm) above the rim (Figure 9a).
Imagine or lightly draw a triangle A_1–A_2–A_3 on
to the surface of the oasis. Push three ears of the
same kind obliquely into the rim of the oasis
below each point (Figure 9b). Now imagine or
lightly draw a second triangle B_1–B_2–B_3, and
insert an ear of another kind into the oasis
below each of these points. Repeat this with a
third triangle, C_1–C_2–C_3. Make sure that all the
ears are of the same length so that the basket,
when made up, will be nice and round.

Now push a good ear of wheat or rye into the
centre of the oasis. You can insert another three
ears obliquely a little away from the centre of
the oasis (Figure 9c).

Now fill the whole piece of oasis *lightly* with
oat-ears 3″–4″ (8–10 cm) high. This grain is
softer and hides the oasis.

Now begin inserting the remaining ears towards the middle, working from below up and
going round all the time. Ears which are hanging
down should of course be facing outwards
(Figure 9d).

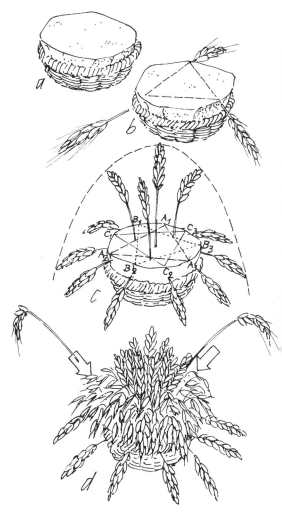

Figure 9.

Figure 10.

Preparations for plaiting

Before the straws are worked they must be *peeled*, that is to say the long thin leaves which often lie closely round the stalk must be removed. This is best done by running a potato-peeler down the stalk from top to bottom. This must be done carefully otherwise the stalk can break at the nodules (Figure 12). Make sure that the leaves are completely removed round the nodules.

By nature dry straws are stiff and not pliable, so that before plaiting they must be soaked. Lay them in a bath or tub with warm water for an hour, weighing them down with a pail or plate so that they lie well covered with water. Only freshly-cut stalks are still pliant enough to be plaited without being first soaked.

Do not leave the straws in the water for too long, as this will affect their quality adversely. So do not soak any more straws than you require for plaiting. You will need some practice before being able to judge how much straw you will need for any particular article. Depending on

the thickness and tightness of the plait, it will be 50% to 60% of the length of the flat straws, so that for each plait you will need two or three times its length of straws.

Figure 12.

Figure 13.

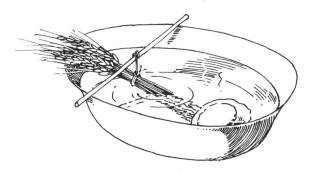

Figure 11.

Plaiting a straw heart

Materials
Waste straw
(the length of the plait is about 26" 66 cm)

Method
Use straws *without* ears. Take them out of the water first cutting off any bits too thin and any nodules at the end of the straws. Although there are various methods of plaiting only the simplest with three straws will be used in this book.

For the straw hearts in Figures 13 and 14 begin with twelve or fifteen straws depending on their thickness. Straws are always thinner at the top than at the bottom; therefore turn some

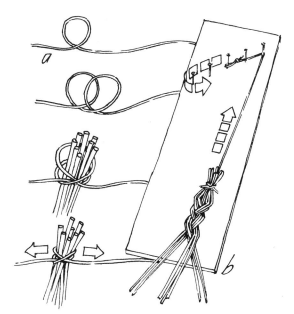

Figure 15.

Figure 14.

of the straws round so that the thickness of the bundle remains even all the way along. In order to get as tight a plait as possible tie the end of the bundle of straws tightly together with string. For this the *clove-hitch* is the most useful knot as it can be drawn tight immediately (see Figure 15a). Then tie an extra knot if necessary. In order to plait tightly tie the other end of the string to something.

For plaiting you can use a "plaiting-board." This is a board about 10" × 32" (25 × 80 cm) which has four nails driven in at one end (Figure 15b). As the plaiting proceeds the string can be wound round the nails so that the actual point of plaiting remains at the same distance from your body.

21

Divide the bundle of straws into three equal parts. As can be seen in Figure 16 first the bundle of straws furthest to the right (C) is brought over the bundle in the middle (B). Then bring the left-hand bundle (A) over bundle (C) which has now become the middle bundle. Then bring the right-hand bundle over the middle one, and so on.

It is important to keep an angle of 90° between the bundles. This gives the best plaiting result.

Often the straws will still be stiff even though they have been soaked. Press the straws together between your thumb and forefinger before the bundle is plaited.

If the straw becomes very dry during the plaiting lay the plait back into the water for five to ten minutes. Tie the loose end of the plait to prevent it coming apart.

Figure 16.

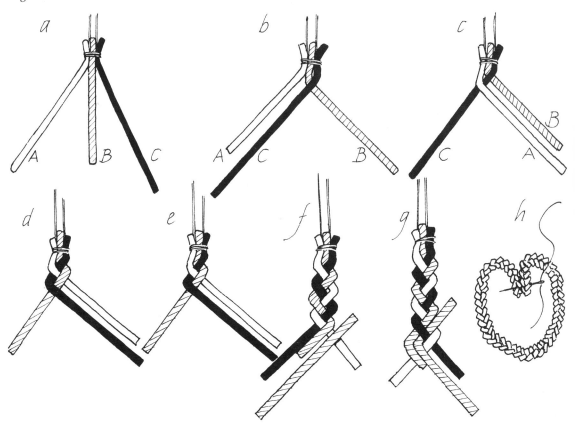

Adding Fresh Straws during the Plaiting

At a particular moment one of the bundles can come to an end before the plait is finished. Stages *f* and *g* on Figure 16 show how to proceed. Lay one or more straws on the remains of the bundle and then fold one of the other bundles over it and so on. It is obvious that you will have a problem if all the bundles come to an end at the same time. To avoid this make sure at the beginning that the bundles are of different lengths. Once the plait is finished cut off all bits of straw that stick out.

Finishing

Tie up the three bundles together once the desired length of plaiting has been achieved. Cut off the remainder of the straws, smooth the wet plait into the required form and sew it up with needle and thread. The plait will require about twenty-four hours in order to dry completely. While it is drying lay something heavy on it (such as a board) to keep it nice and flat. After drying, trim the ends. For decorating and making up plaits see page 9ff.

In the following patterns the length of the plait and the number of straws required is given as a guide, but of course you may vary this.

A double straw heart

Materials
Waste straw
A red ribbon
(the inside heart is about 20½" (52 cm) long;
 the outside heart about 27½" (70 cm) long.

Method
The double straw heart is a variation of the single heart. The method is the same, only the finishing off is different because the hearts are fixed together.

Make two plaits of different lengths. Fold the longer plait over in the middle and sew up the fold with a few stitches. Fold the shorter one over in the middle round the first plait and sew

Figure 17.

it a bit lower down on to the first plait (Figure 18).

Now bend the outside (shortest) plait-ends down to make a heart shape and sew the ends together with a few stitches. Then bend the long inside plait-end round it and sew the ends on to the other heart firmly.

After drying cut off the inside end of the joined hearts and trim the bottom joint neatly. Hang the hearts up with a red ribbon or red wool.

Figure 18.

Plaiting a straw wreath

Materials
Wheat or rye straw
(the length of the plait is 28"–32" (70–80 cm)

Method
With the straw heart the ends were sewn together so that the plaiting was side-on. With a wreath (Figure 19) you see the plaiting head-on and the two ends are laid one over the other. Here a tied-up bundle of straws would not look good at the beginning, so this plaiting is begun in a different way (see Figure 20).

Take a bunch of wet straws (some of which are head to tail to make it even) which is only

Figure 19.

half as thick as necessary. Separate into three bundles, making sure they are of different lengths. Bend them double (see Figure 20).

For the rest the plaiting is the same as that of the straw heart, except that the one end of the wet bent-over plait is laid over the other and the ends are then sewn together tightly (Figure 19). It is important that this plait be dried *under weight* to prevent the circle from setting warped.

Figure 20.

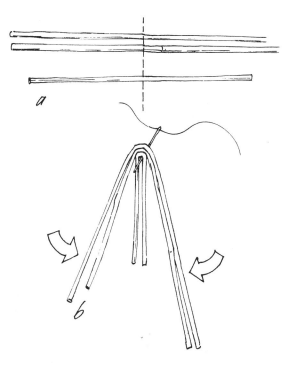

Cross with a wreath of ears

Materials
Wheat or rye straws for the plait-work
Barley with grains in two rows for the wreath of ears
Oat and wheat with chaff-husks for the decoration
(the circumference of the circle is 24″, 62 cm; the length of the cross 8″, 20 cm)

Method
For plaiting the wreath fifteen straws are needed. Plaiting is done in the same way as for the straw wreath (page 24), but now during the plaiting a straw with a barley ear with two rows of grain is added each time on one side. As can be seen in Figure 22 the barley straw is *gripped*

Figure 21.

25

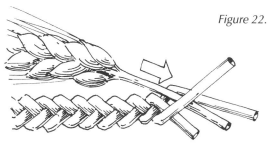

Figure 22.

between the other straws when it is bent over. Make sure that the ear sticks out nicely and does not swing round.

If the bundles become too thick so that the plaiting becomes uneven, cut off the barley straws after a few folds. Barley straws are quite thin so that it may be necessary to strengthen them here and there with thin wire.

Make the cross by sewing one short plait on top of another.

It is best to sew the cross on to the circle after drying. As can be seen on Figure 21 the plaiting is decorated with a round posy, mainly of oats, which accentuates the form of the plait-work.

A plait-work of five hearts

Materials

Wheat or rye straw for the plaiting

Barley ears with grain in two or six rows of grain for the decoration

(the circumference of the wreath is about 25", 63 cm; the length of the plait for the hearts is 18", 46 cm)

Method

Plaiting the hearts

Begin the plaits with nine straws. First make one heart complete (see page 21). This can serve as

a pattern for the other four. Tie up the hearts provisionally so that the heart shape is quite apparent.

Making up the decorations

For decorating the inside we need five bundles of fanned-out barley-straw. The fanning-out is done as follows: take six or seven wet straws without ears about 4½" (12 cm) long, tie them together about a third of the way along and pull the thread tight so that the straws stand out like a fan (see Figure 24). You can use the clove-hitch (see Figure 15a). This is best done with two people, one holding the straws. For sureness tie an extra knot in the thread. Tie up the short end of the fan and cut off the straws neatly just below the tie.

Now sew each heart together, so that the

Figure 23.

fanned-out bundles of barley-straws can be sewn as invisibly as possible between the two ends of the heart. Allow the hearts to dry. Now the hearts can be sewn together. Between the sides of each of two hearts sew a bundle of fanned-out barley-ears which is made in the same way as the bundles of fanned-out straws.

Finally cut the ends of the fans in the centre to the same lengths.

Making the wreath

Once the foundation shape is finished the wreath can be plaited and sewn either on the front or back of the foundation shape as you wish.

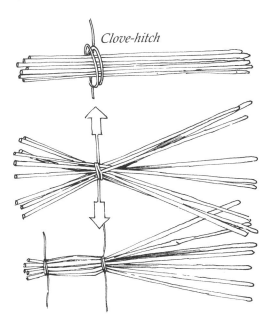

Clove-hitch

Figure 24.

A "sun" made of ears

Materials
Straws or stalks of the same thickness
12 wheat-ears with chaff-husks
Strong thread

Method
Cut wetted straws or stalks in 12 equal lengths of 4″ (10 cm) and iron them flat (with an iron). Lay six straws one on top of the other as in Figure 27, making first a simple saltire cross and then a double saltire cross. The first and last straw now form a cross enclosing the other straws.

The thread which binds the crosses together is passed from behind and goes over the last

Figure 25.

straw, under the next one, and so on. In this way a twelve-pointed star is produced.

With the remaining straws make a second star with twelve points, place one star on top of the other and weave a thread through them. Tie them together and cut off the surplus threads. Then fold over the rays of the star 1¼" (3 cm) from the centre and cut points on the remaining long rays.

Take the twelve ears and cut off the stalk leaving only a stem of about ½" (1 cm). Place a bit of glue on it. Now take the rays, which have been ironed flat and cut short, between your thumb and forefinger and one by one press them open again and insert the stem of the ear into them. Hang this splendid sun up in a place where the chaff-husks can also be seen to advantage.

Figure 26.

Variation:
In the sun in Figure 26 twenty-four ears are used instead of twelve with alternately a larger and smaller ear.

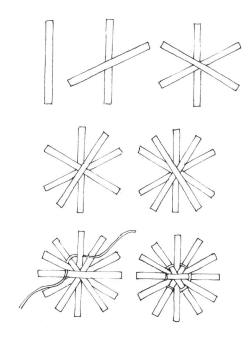

Figure 27.

3 Decorative Straw-Plaiting

A corn-dolly from Wales

Materials
Wheat-straws with ears

Method
This is a very decorative plait which does need some practice to make it really beautifully. It is worth practising with straws which are not so good.

Tie three wet-wheat straws with ears (A, B and C) together just below the ears and fan them out. Now add two new straws D and E as shown in Figure 28a. The new straws are kept in place by bending straws A and C round them (Figure 28b).

In Figure 28c the basic technique is shown clearly: straw B goes over straw A and under straw C and thus comes into the middle on top of the other straws; then it goes under the other

Figure 28.

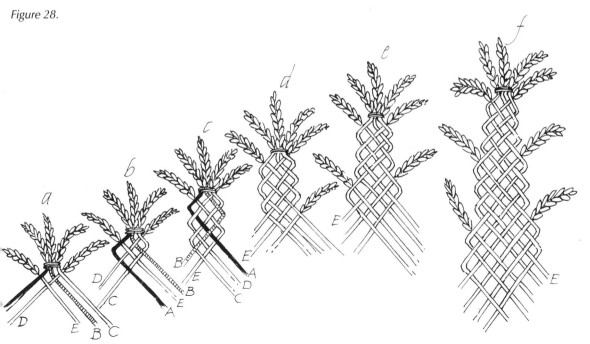

straws right to the edge of the plait. You can see the same thing happening with straw E in Figures 28d and 28e. In order to give the ears plenty of room we fold the straws twice over each time at both sides of the plait before adding a new straw.

You can determine the length of the plait yourself. The corn-dolly in Figure 29 consists of twenty-five straws with ears and is 14" (35 cm) long altogether.

A straw decoration with four-straw plaits

Materials
Eight wheat-straws with ears
Straws for lengthening
Red ribbon

Method
Four-straw plaiting results in a three-dimensional "rope," rather than a flat braid. Tie four wet straws (A, B, C and D) together just below the ears with stout thread and point them in four directions. Now fold straw A towards B and straw B to the place where A was (see Figure 30b). Then fold straw C to D and straw D to the place where C was. Begin again with A

Figure 29.

Figure 30.

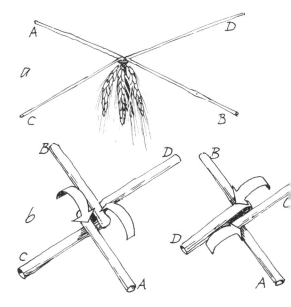

and B and then with C and D. Continue in this way until the plait is about 7" (18 cm) long and then tie the four straws together so that the plaiting does not come apart. Let the unplaited straws just hang for the moment; they should be about 8" (20 cm) long.

Make another plait with four fresh straws. Tie the two plaits together just below the ears. Form them into a heart by tying the other ends together, leaving the unplaited straws pointing down (Figure 31). Tie the unplaited straws with the ears together and cut them off obliquely a bit short of the ears. Arrange the ears so that the plaiting looks nice and adorn it if desired with a piece of coloured ribbon.

To lengthen the straws:

On page 23 we described how you can add new straws during the plaiting. With the four-straw plait (and with spirals described below) this method cannot be used because we are plaiting with single straws and there would be a break in the plait when one straw comes to an end. Whenever working with single straws the straws themselves must be lengthened. This is quite simple.

Generally the end of the straw is thick. If a straw ends with a nodule, cut it off. Then find a second straw with a thinner end and insert it into the opening of the old straw pushing it in until it sticks (Figure 32). Do not push it further to avoid splitting the outside straw. Take care when bending over the lengthened straw. This method of lengthening the straw can of course be used in other cases.

Figure 31.

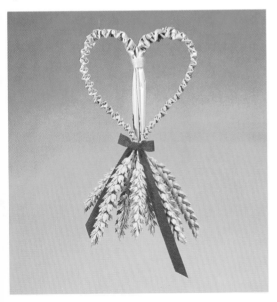

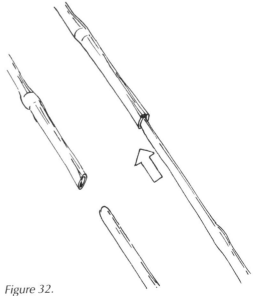

Figure 32.

Straw-plaiting with spirals

Materials
Thin long straws
Thread

Method
This kind of plaiting which originates in England
has various forms with innumerable variations.
It is exacting work which must be done with
care and patience to ensure even plaiting. Do
not be tempted to work too quickly, for the
plaiting will become too loose and untidy and
this is only noticeable when it is too late to do
anything about it.

Because they have to be completely folded
over it is important to use straws which are
pliant, and not too thick. The upper part of the
stalks are best. If a stalk has too many nodules
problems can arise when it is bent over sharply,
for it can break at the nodule or protrude, thus
spoiling the regular shape of the spiral. While
plaiting keep a watch for nodules approaching.
If necessary cut the straw before the nodule and
lengthen it as described on page 31. Take care
that the plaiting remains taut while you are
extending the straw.

The satisfying thing about plaiting with spirals
is that while you are working you can decide
whether to widen or narrow the plait, or keep to
the same width.

Spiral plaiting is always three-dimensional.
Although the technique remains the same you
can make plaiting with three, four or more
corners according to the number of straws
used.

Figure 33.

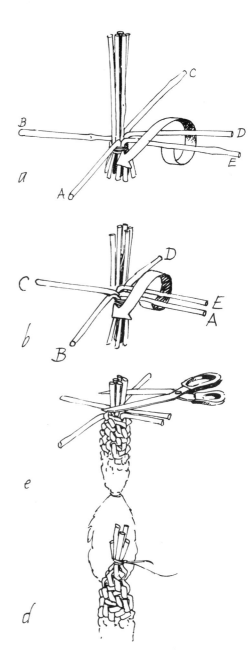

Spiral plaiting with "padding"

For the models in this book we start with plaits with four corners. For this five straws are required. Plaiting *with padding* is easier because the padding gives support during plaiting. So practise first with this. In general the plaiting should form a kind of long tube and so is less amenable to adaptation than the plaitings without padding described later.

Take a bundle of straws, not necessarily all with ears, the minimum number being ten. The width of the plait will be affected by the number of straws. In the pattern in Figure 34 ten straws with ears are used.

Tie up the straws together just below the ears. Take the bundle in one hand and turn the

Figure 34.

straws upside down so that the ears are pointing down and the stalks up. Bend five straws on the outside of the bundle so that they are pointing out horizontally in four directions (see Figure 33a), with the fourth and fifth straws, D and E pointing to your right. The remaining straws form the padding. With your free hand work straw E under D and then back over D so that it lands up on straw A (Figure 33b). Then move the plait a quarter-turn anticlockwise so that now straws A and E are pointing to the right. Now work straw A under and over E to come to rest by B. Repeat this procedure until the plait has nearly reached the desired length and the straws have become quite short. Now cut the padding off (Figure 33c) and plait one or two more rows whereby the plait becomes smaller and the padding disappears. Then tie the five plaited straws directly under the plait together (Figure 33d).

Finally cut off the tied straws evenly and if desired adorn the plait with a coloured bow. If the ears make too big a bunch, cut a few off.

Spiral plaiting without "padding"

As soon as you have acquired some skill in plaiting *with padding* you should now be able to succeed in making spiral plaiting which is hollow. Take special care that the plait remains taut.

The principle has already been described but this kind of plaiting allows the spiral form to become wider or narrower. Bringing straw E next to A (as in Figure 33a), but leaving a little gap before laying straw A over E, allows the plait to become wider as in the spiral in Figure 34. If E lies *on top of* A the plait will retain the same width. If E lies over A (that is to the left of A) then the plait will become narrower again.

Variation: cup-shaped plaiting
If you make a spiral plait that is *open* at the bottom do not make the plait narrower at the end finishing in a point, but finish it off when it has the desired length and is still quite open.

Finishing off is done as follows: with the last row secure each straw with thread to the straw beside it. Then cut off the bit of straw sticking out.

A mobile of straw spirals

In Figure 35 you can see a variety of plaits. Of course you can also use straws with ears.

The hangers of the mobile in this case are of copper-wire, while the spirals are hung up by red woollen yarn to add a bit of colour.

Figure 35.

34

4 Straw Figures

A straw billy-goat (Yule-buck)

Materials
About 25 straws 18″ (45 cm) long and 30 straws
12″ (30 cm) long
Thin wire (bouquet or florist's wire)
Copper wire
Straw-coloured or other coloured thread

Method
This straw billy-goat (or Yule-Buck) comes from
Sweden. Although the number and the length
of the straws are given this is only a guide and
can be varied.

Wet straw is easily pliant and it can be dried
in its bent form. For the goat described here the
straw has to be bent quite considerably and so it
is good to use some wire to hold the straw in the
correct form.

Begin with the *horns*. For these select two lots
of 3 straws which are not too thick and have a
long stretch without nodules. Insert into at least
two of the three straws a piece of very thin wire
(Figure 37a), tie the three straws together and
make a plait of about 6″ (15 cm). Roll up the
plait (Figure 37b) and secure it, but do not cut
off the unplaited ends. Because of the wire
plaited with the straw the horns will remain in
the required shape.

Repeat the above for the second horn.

Then take 20 to 25 of the 18″ (45 cm) straws
for the goat's head, neck and body. Lay the

straws alternately head to tail so that the thin
ends are evenly distributed. Insert the copper
wire into two straws. If there is a nodule in the
straw push the copper wire in from both ends
up to the nodule. Now tie the bundle together
at one end (clove-hitch with a few extra knots,
see Figure 15a), and fold it over about 1½″ (3–4
cm) from the end. Then insert the horns into the
bundle (the goat's neck) and secure as shown in
Figure 37e. Now fill the bundle by inserting a
further five to eight straws. Fold over the bundle

Figure 36.

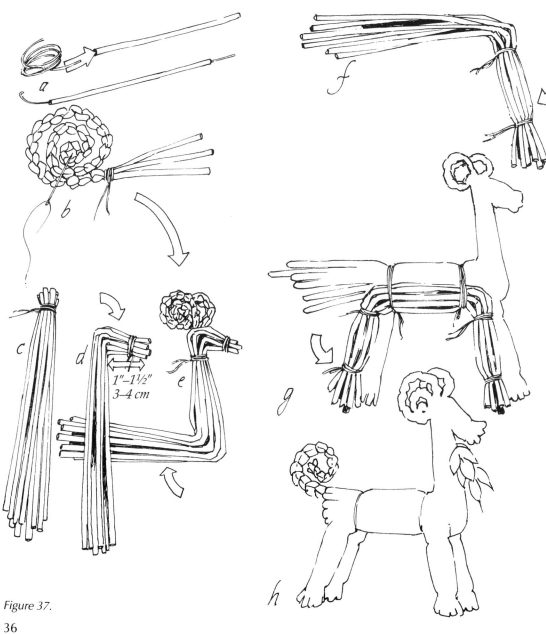

1"–1½"
3–4 cm

Figure 37.

once more to make the body and this can now be secured. The wire will hold the bundle of straws in the required shape.

For the goat's legs we need twice 15 straws about 12" (30 cm) long. Again insert copper wire into two straws so that the bundle will stand in the right shape. Tie up the forelegs in two places (Figure 37f) and now make the second bundle similarly. Fold the two bundles to make them part of the goat's body (Figure 37g) and secure behind the forelegs, passing the thread a couple of times round the body before tying. Add a few straws if the body is too thin. Now fold the leg bundles over to make the hindlegs and tie them up in two places (Figure 36).

From the unfinished end of the head-and-body piece select six straws to plait into a tail after inserting two thin wires into the straws. Then trim the remaining straws. Roll up the plaited tail and trim the legs.

Bend the horns into a good shape and stick a little bundle of oat-heads or grasses as a tuft below the head in the neck. Now go over all the knots and cut off the loose threads, if necessary putting a touch of glue on the ends.

A straw cock

Materials
Straws
Oat-straws or dried grasses
Thin wire
Copper wire
Thread of various colours

Method
Using damp straw make two plaits, each with three straws. The plait should be about 2½" (6–7 cm) long, with loose straw at both ends extending another 1¼" (3 cm). Tie each plait into a loop. They make the gills of the cock (Figure 39a).

For the cock's comb make three plaits of equal length, but plait only the middle of the straws, leaving about 8" (20 cm) at each end of the plait. Tie these plaits into loops.

For the head-and-body piece we need fifteen straws about 14" (35 cm) long. The method is roughly the same as that for the straw billy-goat (page 35). When tying the head tie in the plaited gills (Figure 38) and tie in the plaited comb into the neck at the same time.

For the legs we need about twelve straws about 9" (22 cm). Try to select straws without nodules. Insert thin wire into three straws and lay these apart. Insert the thicker copper wire into two other straws.

Now make the toes at the ends of the straws. Because they tend to split when bent over, exposing the wire inside, the ends are finished off with a whipping, which is done as follows (Figure 39).

Place one of the straws (which were laid apart) with wire in it and one plain straw together. Lay a loop of the thread over the end of the straw and pass the long end of the thread round the loop and round both straws (Figure 39c). Now wind the thread tightly round the loop and both straws until the binding is about ³/₈″ (8–10 mm) wide. Push the end A through the loop (Figure 39d) and pull the thread tight. By pulling B the loop will disappear below the binding. Cut off the visible end A, pull it right under the binding and cut off the end B.

Repeat this whipping at the other end of the two straws, and then make two more bundles of two straws tied at each end. You now have three lengths of double straw (one plain and one with wire) with each end whipped. You have used six of your twelve straws. Put these six and the remaining six together into a bundle of twelve straws. Tie the bundle at each end about ¼″ (5 mm) from the whippings. Bend the

Figure 38.

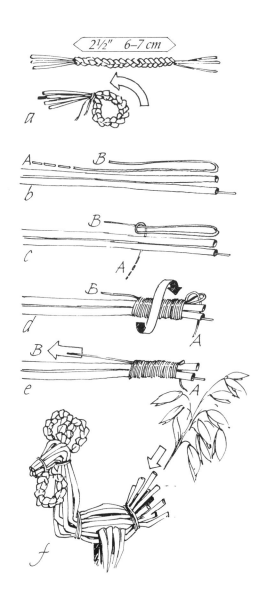

Figure 39.

bundle round to make a U, insert it into the body of the cock and tie it in.

Now bend the tail up from the body. The wire in the straws will ensure that the straws maintain their shape. Because the rest will dry into shape tie up the tail into one bundle and allow the cock to dry.

When the cock is dry cut the tie, and the straws of the tail should fan out. They may need smoothing down here and there. Cut the tail straws one by one to different lengths. For the tail of the cock in Figure 38 wild oats were used. These sometimes grow at the edge of the fields and have no seeds (the seeds would make the tail too heavy). Alternatively use various grasses. Apply a little glue to the ends of the oat-straws or grasses inserted into the tail. Continue with this until you have an ample tail.

Now we come to the *toes* of the feet. Bend the whipped toes into the right shape (two toes to the front, and one to the back) and cut off the surplus straw at the "ankle." If you leave the thick copper wire in place you can make the cock stand by inserting the wire into two holes in a piece of bark or wood.

To finish off you can of course use a spray with some water-colour to give the oats or grasses some colour.

A horse of plaited straw

Materials
12 straws
Button-thread
Single ears

Method
This horse is made completely of plaited straw (Figure 40). The horse shown below is plaited from twelve straws. To add fresh straws to the plaiting see Figures 16f-g. As the plait becomes thicker the animal becomes bigger and the plaits longer. It is not so easy to determine the exact proportions of the horse. It can be a help to draw the horse to scale on a piece of paper. Figure 41f shows the measurements for the horse in Figure 40.

Figure 40.

Begin by plaiting the legs. Figure 16 shows how to plait the straw, but for the legs the plait has to make a bend (see Figures 41a-d). Normally (as in Figure 41a) strand A is passed over B, but to make a bend to the left, C goes over B and then under A (Figure 41b). Then B is passed over A. After that you continue in the normal way.

First plait two legs with two bends and secure them to part of the under-body (Figure 41e). Fold the ends of the legs over and sew up (Figure 41f), giving short, straight legs. Then plait the head, neck and body of the horse, folding the head double and sewing up into the correct shape. It can often be a help to lay the plait once more in water to make it pliant.

Sew the horse together with button-thread as in Figure 41g. Using zigzag stitches will make the sewing unobtrusive. If the horse does not have a good shape, soak it and reshape before allowing it to dry. You can use some wire wound round the legs, body and head to keep the animal in shape while drying.

Once the horse has been completely sewn

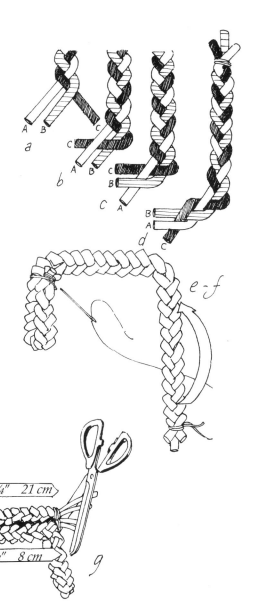

Figure 41.

together you can cut off the straws sticking out at the tail.

Now the horse has to be finished off and that is a laborious and exacting job.

For the ears and mane use a few ears of grain. First make some holes with a thick needle and stick the stems of the grain-ears in (using glue if necessary).

Finally insert single ears of grain (or grasses) in the cut-off straws at the tail and glue them in.

Dolls of plaited straw

Materials
9–12 long straws
Thread of various colours

Method
Depending on the thickness of the straws take nine to twelve straws for the plait. Tie the straws together 4″ (10 cm) from the end. Plait the long end of the straws to a length of about 4½″ (12 cm). Tie up the plait and fold double (Figure 43a). About ¾″–1″ (2 cm) from the fold tie both parts of the plait together with button-thread. This makes the neck. (The button-thread is strong enough to make the neck narrower than the head.)

Now plait the arms. As shown in Figure 42 two methods of plaiting are used: the women have arms of the usual plait and the men have four-straw plaited arms. With the women's arms you can see the difference between thick and thin straws. Make the arms 4″ (10 cm) long and tie them up well at both sides. Place the arms between the two ends of the large plait directly below the "neck" (Figure 43b).

Now tie up the waist at the place where the two ends of the plait are tied together. Do this also with button-thread to obtain a narrower waist.

The lower body of the woman consists of unplaited straws about 3″ (7 cm) long. In its present form it is still too thin, so lay some bits of straw — preferably without nodules — round the waist, hold them tight with one hand and tie these straws with the other hand firmly to the waist. Figure 43d shows how the doll then appears. Now fold down the straws which are sticking up at the waist. Because these straws which form the skirt tend not to stay in place tie them together loosely from under the skirt, after which lay the doll for some minutes in water. Allow the doll to dry and then release the tie; the straws should then nearly always stay down. As shown in Figure 42 one of the women has an "apron" because the straws which were pointing up and have been folded down have been cut off shorter and tied down with a coloured thread.

For the man, divide the unplaited straws of the lower body in two after tying up the waist, plait the two halves into legs and tie them at the ends.

It should be easy to get the women to stand; with the men this is more difficult, but if the feet are trimmed properly you should get them to stand; you can also plait a bit of copper wire into the two legs, leaving the wire to protrude a bit and insert it into a bit of bark.

For the baby use some left-over straws, fold them into two and tie them up. Of course the body can also be plaited and you can clothe the dolls with little bits of cloth or dried leaves.

Figure 42.

The basket is made of a plait of three ears. As shown in Figure 42 the plaits are sewn together with thread to make a basket. Of course bigger baskets and boxes can be made in the same way by using more straws.

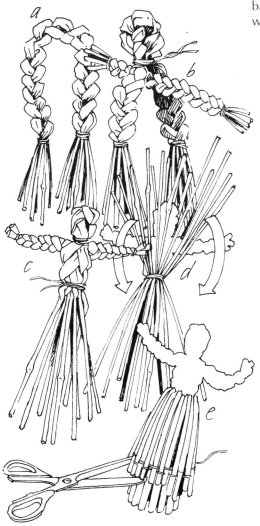

Figure 43.

5 Corn-Husk Dolls

Corn (maize) husks were used by the Indians to make baskets, rugs and playthings. The colonists of the New World learned their skills and passed these back to Europe, where particularly the Czechs are known for their meticulously crafted dolls.

The husks of the corn cob make up the basic material for these dolls. In summer maize-cobs are readily available. If you cannot obtain corn-cobs with covering leaves find a farmer who grows maize and ask him for a few cobs.

Because the husks are brittle the cobs must be "peeled" carefully. Cut the husks round the stalk (Figure 44). Remove the fuzzy silks carefully from the top of the cob, and dry them well in the sun (if they are not quite dry they can go mouldy). They will shortly come in handy to use as hair.

The fine, thin husks of the cob are best dried in a flower-press or a telephone book with a weight on it, To make them nice and flat. If they are dried in the sun they tend to curl up. If the leaves have a yellowish green colour after being dried, lay them out in the sun and the greenish colour will be bleached away.

The rough, brittle husks of the plant itself can be dried in the sun, and will be used as stuffing.

The dried husks look and can be cut like paper. It is a fine material, so try to lay in a good store during the harvest.

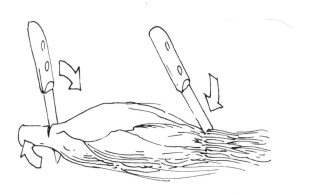

Figure 44.

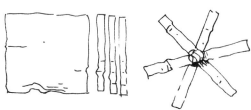

Figure 45.

Materials

Husks of the corn-cob
Dried corn silks
Balls of cotton-wool, cork or polystyrene with a
    diameter of $3/8''$–$1''$ (8–24 mm)
Cotton wool
Very thin wire
Copper wire $1/32''$ (0.8 mm)
Button-hole thread in various suitable colours
Glue
A large needle or awl
Pair of scissors

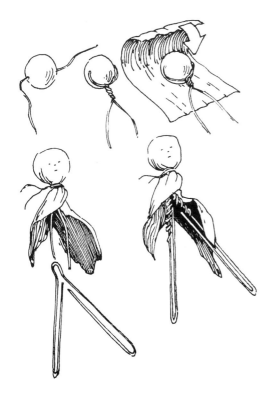

Figure 46.

Method

Although the husks are first dried they can generally only be worked when they are moistened to make them pliant. Dry husks have the tendency to break.

Lay only a few husks in a basin of lukewarm water for five minutes. Note that wet husks expand and shrink again when they are drying.

The head

For corn-husk dollies begin with the head. For this we need a little ball as padding which can be of cotton-wool, cork or polystyrene, or even a round wooden bead. If none of these is available cut up a dry husk into strips about $1/4''$ (5 mm). Cut along the width, that is across the veins. Make a little ball out of these strips as shown in Figure 45. Stick the ends of the strips together with a bit of glue. The biggest dolls shown here have a head with a diameter of about $1''$ (25 mm).

With a strong needle or an awl make a hole right through the ball and push a piece of wire right through. Twist the ends together (Figure 46c). The wire must not be too short for we shall need it to strengthen the body.

Now select a good thin (but not too wide) wet husk. Put the ball in the middle and wrap one side of the leaf over the ball. Make sure that the wire passes from the one ear past the chin to the other ear.

Now wrap the leaf round the ball with as few folds as possible, keeping the folds to one side of the ball — the back of the head. With buttonhole-thread wrap the leaf as tightly as possible round the neck and secure. Wind the thread four or five times round the neck and secure. This gives the doll a neck and the head

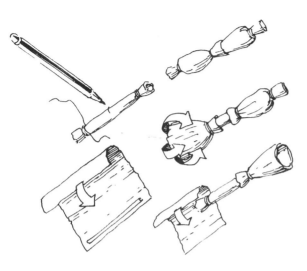

$2\frac{1}{2}''$ (6×6 cm). As shown in Figure 47 the sleeves are puckered and tied inside out to the arms, then turned outside in and secured in the middle of the arms. If the sleeves do not puff out, fill them with some left-over husks.

Now secure the arms to the head, making sure that a bit of the neck still shows. Choose the side of the head with the least folds to make into the face. Fix the arms to the back of the neck by criss-crossing some thread round them and securing.

Figure 47.

Figure 48.

does not run straight into the body. The rest of the maize-leaf is left to hang (Figure 46e).

The arms:
For the doll's arms take a piece of copper wire (or thin wires twisted together) about 4'' (10 cm) long. Wrap a piece of maize-leaf round the wire. The leaf should stick out about $\frac{1}{2}''$ (1 cm) at each end and should be about 3'' (7–8 cm) long depending on the thickness of the leaf (a thin leaf needs to be wrapped more times round otherwise the arms look too thin). Tie up the rolled-up leaf *just beyond each end of the wire* (Figure 47). Mark the middle of the arms with a pen. Now give the arms sleeves; the women a half or three-quarter sleeve, the men long sleeves. For this use a maize-leaf $2\frac{1}{2}'' \times$

The upper body

Now fill the body and the back. For this tie two narrow husks (about 1¼″, 3 cm wide) to the middle of the neck immediately above the arms (Figure 49b). Fill the back where the arms are secured with a little ball of cotton-wool. For the stomach take half a ball of cotton-wool or cork of the same size as the head. Fold the strips of tied-on maize-leaf over the cotton-wool and the half-ball and tie them at the waist with thread.

To finish off the shoulders cut a few husk strips about ½″ (10–15 mm) wide. Lay one of the strips obliquely from the left shoulder to the right side of the waist and secure there. Repeat for the other side (Figure 49d). Repeat this again if the side of the upper body is not quite covered. Finally do this once more, fastening the strips more loosely round the upper body, so that when they dry and shrink they do not fit too tightly round the body. These last strips form the blouse.

The lower body

Now comes the lower body. For a man make legs and trousers. For this the two ends of the wire are wrapped separately with husks and tied at top and bottom (Figs. 49e-f). Then bend the ends of the legs to make a foot. Now make the trousers by wrapping husks round the legs until they are thick enough. The last husk is cut and the top wound round the upper body. If necessary stick husk with glue when it is dry.

To make more baggy trousers, wrap a puckered husk loosely round the leg and secure it only at the thigh. If you wish to give the doll knickerbockers make these in the same way as for the puff-sleeves, but first secure the husk at

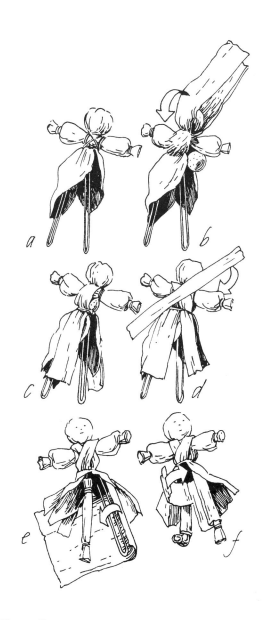

Figure 49.

47

the "ankle," turn it inside out and secure it at the thighs.

You can cover all rough ends and loose bits by giving the doll a smock (Figure 51).

The lower body of the women can be filled, or simply consist of a skirt and petticoat.

For a filled lower body you can take left-over husks. Cut them into strips, wet them and lay the out as a fan and place the doll on its back in the middle of it. Now secure the strips to the waist (Figure 50a). Repeat this with the doll lying on its front. Now fold the husks above the waist down, and tie them together.

Select one or two good (damp) husks and wrap the whole doll up in them, securing them at the waist, bending the arms up beside the head (Figure 50c). Fold the top half of the husk down and smooth it. Trim the bottom of the skirt so that the doll can stand. With this filled skirt it is important that the husks inside are really dry to avoid their going mouldy. To dry the doll put it near a radiator for a few days.

If you are making a doll with a lower body that is not filled, and which has only a skirt and petticoat then just follow the instructions for the last maize-leaves. Take care that the skirt flounces out well and is firm so that the doll will stand. The advantage of this skirt is that you can bend the doll's legs and she can sit or kneel. Make sure that the wire is not visible.

Figure 50.

48

Finishing off

Once the dolls have been thoroughly dried trim all the edges of the maize-leaves and secure all the loose thread with glue. The dolls can now be dressed with dry husks which can be cut and can be stuck on. Use the curly silks for hair. They can be plaited if moistened.

Husks can be coloured by fabric dying or batik. However, it is very laborious for the husks used, and we shall not describe it further here.

The soft tints of the skirts of the dolls shown in Figures 48 and 51 were obtained by laying the husks in a basin of fairly concentrated water-colours for half an hour, and then rinsing them in clean water. Dry the husks afterwards in a flower-press. You can also colour the husks with a spray before cutting out the clothing.

It is also possible to colour the finished doll with a paintbrush and water-colours.

Figure 51.

6 Harvest Materials from Woods and Fields

On page 11 you can see some of the things which can be found in autumn. Mostly they can be picked from the ground, without harming any trees or plants. For instance, chestnuts, Spanish chestnuts, acorns, beech-nuts, pine-cones, fir-cones, corn on the cob and corn silks, hazelnuts, rosehips, little feathers, maple seeds, lime-tree seeds, honesty pennies, and so on, can provide hours of imaginative play for young children.

Let me repeat that the figures and models given in this book are meant to give you ideas and to stimulate your own creativity, and need not be slavishly copied.

Keep the collection of materials in a dry place with plenty of air. Take care especially with chestnuts and acorns that they do not go mouldy (so do not keep them in a plastic bag). You can store different kinds of cereals, grasses and tassels in tall glasses. For other materials simple cardboard trays are handy.

A cardboard storage tray

Materials
Stout paper or thin card (8½" × 11", A4, or larger)

Method
Fold the paper or card in half and half again once along the long side and once on the short side (Figure 52). Raise the long sides first, then raise one of the short sides, fold the corner inwards and glue it together. Fold the overlapping piece to the short side inwards and stick it with a bit of glue. Do the same with the other short side and the tray is finished.

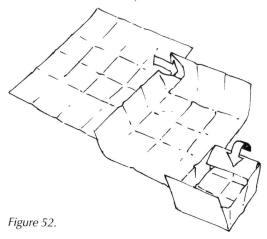

Figure 52.

Dolls and animals from chestnuts, acorns and other materials

Materials

Spanish and ordinary chestnuts
Acorns
Grains of corn (maize), corn husks and silks
Hazelnuts
Beech-nut husks
Rosehips
Cocktail sticks or wooden barbecue-skewers
Copper wire
A straw
Sunflower seeds
Sycamore or maple seeds

Method

Select a few good chestnuts of the right proportions for the head and body parts of the person. With an awl or bodkin (or even a darning needle) make holes in the chestnuts and join them together with a piece of a cocktail stick. Insert a piece of copper wire for the arms at the right height in the upper body (first boring a hole if necessary). The upper part of the arms can be made of acorns which should be bored beforehand; the lower part of the arms are made of maize-grains, threaded on to the copper wire, and the hands are made of little bits of straw. The wire enables you to bend the arms. Make the legs from cocktail sticks inserted firmly into holes bored in the chestnut. Cut an acorn lengthwise through the middle to make a pair of shoes.

Figure 53.   Figure 54.

51

The woman in Figure 53 is finished off with an apron made from a corn husk and some hair made from the silks. The man has an acorn hat and smokes an acorn pipe.

The dog is made of two acorns, a pair of sunflower seeds for his ears (cut slits in the head for the ears) and cocktail sticks.

The materials used for the dolls in Figure 54 are self-evident. The basket on the woman's arm is made of half a walnut and the handle from a strip of corn husk.

The sprig of honesty-pennies in the background stands in a disc cut from a branch.

For the dolls in Figure 55 acorn-cups, a shell from a chestnut and rosehips as well as other things are used.

In Figure 56 flat chestnuts or half acorns are used for the birds to prevent them from falling over.

To make the wings use sycamore or maple seed wings.

Figure 55.

Figure 56.

52

A snake made of acorns

Materials
Acorns
A rosehip
A red autumn leaf
Copper wire

Method
Bore a little hole lengthwise in the acorn and thread the acorn on to the copper wire. Do not make the holes too big — the acorns should sit tightly on the wire.

For the eyes use two tiny pieces of rosehip peel, glue them on to sockets previously made in the head.

Finally insert into the little cut-open mouth a good firm red autumn leaf (Figure 57).

Figure 57.

A pine-cone owl

Materials
A pine-cone
Pine-needles
Two acorn-cups with stems
A beech-nut
Sycamore or maple seed wings

Method
With a piece of sandpaper flatten the bottom of the pine-cone, so that the owl will not fall over. Take single sycamore or maple seed wings, cut off the thick seed leaving only the wings. Stick three wings together to make each foot for the owl. When the feet are dry, glue them to the bottom of the pine-cone (Figure 58).

With an awl, bodkin or thick needle make a

Figure 58.

hole in the beech-nut and thread a piece of fine wire (florist's wire) through it to secure the beech-nut (the owl's beak) between the scales of the pine-cone.

Bind the stalks of the acorn-cups together with fine wire and then using the same wire secure the two cups between the scales of the pine-cone so that the beak fits nicely between the two acorn-cup eyes. If necessary remove some of the scales to get the eyes into their proper place.

Finally take a pine twig and secure it to the top of the pine-cone (with fine wire).

Pine-cone mice

Materials
Pointed pine-cones
Dried lime-tree seeds
Corn silks or strips of moss

Method
The mice shown in Figure 59 are very simple to make. Select very pointed pine-cones with the scales still closed. Make a little hole in the bottom where the stalk joins and glue in the tail which can be made from various materials, for instance wet silks twisted into a thin streamer, strands of moss or simply a thin strip of leather or a piece of wool. The glued-on eyes can be made from a tiny twig, as with the smallest mouse; or as with the other mice, from half a lime seed. On the tree these seeds have a grey-green colour, but when dry they harden and turn almost black.

Figure 59.

Winged creatures

Materials
Pine-cones
Larch-cones
Acorns with cups
Feathers
Beech-nuts
Maple seeds
Lime-tree seeds with wings
Small downy feathers

Method
The birds in Figure 60 have pine-cone or fir-cone bodies. For the heads various materials are used; an acorn with cup and stalk, a little pine-cone or larch-cone with stalk. Fasten them to the body by their stalks or with a twig and glue them on, boring a hole first if necessary.

For the wings and tail various materials are used: the wings of lime-tree seeds, the wings of maple or sycamore seeds and little downy feathers. Especially the hanging birds of Figure 61 can fly because they have real down feathers.

Variation:
Make a number of *flying* birds and assemble them to make a *bird-mobile*, as with the plaited spirals in Figure 35 or attach them to a hoop as with the bee-mobile in Figure 63.

Figure 60.

Figure 61.

A pine-cone decoration

Materials
A pine-cone
All sorts of grasses, plant tassels (panicles), and
    so on

Method
Select a nice round pine-cone and stick on all
kinds of grasses and tassels (panicles) between
the scales in a circle round it. It is best not to try
to stick everything on at once, but to work layer
by layer, looking all the while to see where
something can be added in order to keep a
harmonious appearance.

First stick on a number of well-spaced grasses
and allow them to dry before proceeding. This
drying is best done by placing the pine cone in
an egg-cup allowing the stalks of the grasses to
rest on the rim.

Once the first ring has dried you can start
putting in and gluing the next.

A pine-cone as a weather-indicator

Tie a pine-cone to a thread and hang it up in a
shady place outside in front of the window
where you can see it from inside the house. If
the air is damp the scales will draw together,
and in dry warm weather they will open. In this
way the pine-cone indicates humidity and
shows what the weather is going to be.

An acorn spinning-top

Materials
Acorns
A piece of cardboard
Cocktail-sticks

Method
Select a round acorn with a little point, and
make a hole in the bottom.

From a piece of stout cardboard cut out a
disc with a diameter of 2"–2½" (5–6 cm)
depending on the size of the acorn. Colour one
side of the disc. Then make a hole in the middle
of the disc, inserting a cocktail-stick through the
hole in the disk and thrust it into the hole in the
acorn. Make sure that the holes are exactly in
the centre and that the cocktail-stick is firmly
secured in the acorn. Now the top is finished
and while spinning the colours make interesting
patterns. If the colours are circular or spiral they
will have a greater effect.

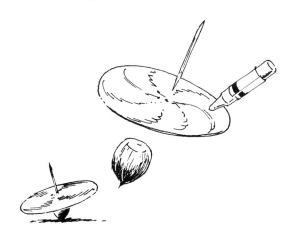

Figure 62.

A bee-mobile

Materials
Alder-cones
Maple seeds
A piece of rattan (cane)

Method
Cut off the seed-globules from the maple seed wings and glue the wings into the alder cones. Tie a thin thread round the middle of the bees so that they can fly.

Make a hoop from a bit of rattan. If the rattan is too pliant take two canes gluing or tying the two ends together.

Now hang the bees up at different heights on to the hoop (Figure 63).

Figure 63.

A bee

Materials
Conifer cones
Pine-cone seeds

Method
The seeds of the pine-cone are under the scales. As soon as the scales open in warmth the seeds fall out. They are very thin and small. So it may be necessary to use tweezers to stick them on to the conifer cones. These cones also only open fully when it is warm or when they have fallen off the tree and are completely dry.

The bee in Figure 64 has been set on a disc of wood with a little bit of string, so that it is flying over the flower.

Figure 64.

A teasel-head spider

Materials
A teasel

Method
A scary spider can be made from the long lower prickles of a teasel. First cut off the stalk completely, then cut out the spider and hang it up on a thread (Figs 65 and 66).

A teasel hedgehog

Materials
A teasel
Lime-tree seed-cups

Method
You may be lucky and see a hedgehog with young ones following in a line behind: father hedgehog, mother hedgehog and then the baby hedgehogs.

Cut off some of the stalk of the teasel but leave about ¼″ (5 mm) for its nose. Cut away the long spidery bits round the snout and make one side flat by cutting away the prickles with a pair of scissors.

Cut a few dried black lime-tree seeds through the middle: one half is for the snout, two other halves are stuck on for the eyes.

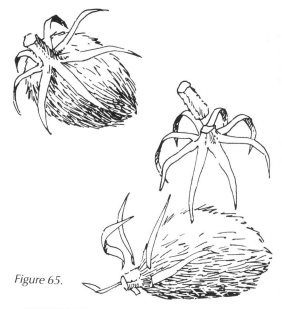

Figure 65.

Figure 66.

58

Tree-spirits

When walking through the woods or on a seashore, it can happen that suddenly in an old piece of weathered wood or a strange twisted root you see a face looking or two figures playing with each other. For children these may become companion tree-spirits whom they would like to take home. Some of these are shown here (Figures 67 and 68). They are ready as you find them and need no crafting.

Pine-cone trolls

Materials
Hazelnut cups
Pine-cones and fir-cones
Corn (maize) silks
Alder-cones
Fine wire

Method
Select a few suitable hazelnut cups and look carefully to see which side looks most like a face. Tie a piece of fine wire between the wild "hairs" of the nut cups so as to be able to tie the head on to the body of a pine-cone.

For the bodies of the two trolls in Figure 70 a

Figure 67.

Figure 68.

pine-cone and a fir-cone are used. Cut off the tops of the pine-cones to make a flat top. Turn the cones upside-down and the flat top now becomes a base and the cones will stand. If necessary secure what is now the bottom row with a bit of beeswax or a bit of clay.

Tie the head on to the pine-cone body with fine wire between the scales so that it cannot be seen (Figure 69a).

For the arms you can use alder-cones, inserting them with their twigs between the scales of the pine-cone and gluing them in.

If there is any wire left over after attaching the head to the body use it for the arms by winding some maize-hair round the wire.

For the feet you can use pine-scales gluing them on or tying them with fine wire, threading them on to the wire first before attaching them to the body. You can also fill up the hollow space at the feet with some clay to get the troll to stand better.

The feet of the smallest troll were made from a piece of pine-cone which had been nibbled away by squirrels.

Figure 70.

Figure 69.

60

Moss-trolls

Materials
Pine-cones
Alder-cones
A hazelnut
Lime-tree seed-cups
Moss and/or maize-silks

Method
Glue two pine-cones together as in Figure 69b. Stick half a hazelnut (the nose) and two lime-tree seed-cups (the eyes) on to the upper pine-cone to make a face and stick two twigs with alder-cones as feet on to the lower pine-cone. The hands of this troll are "invisible."

Make a really ancient troll by dressing him in strips of moss or corn silks (Figure 71).

Figure 71.

Autumn garlands

Autumn garlands can be made using all sorts of materials. While you are out walking in the country have a good look round to see what can be found in the way of ripe fruits and seeds. Suitable materials are: fresh grains of corn (maize) and silks, dried leaves, rosehips, beech-nuts and their husks, acorns and acorn-cups, chestnuts, hazelnuts, straws, Spanish chestnut conker-husks, pumpkin seeds, hop-cones and so on.

Garlands for windows

Depending on what materials you have collected you can adorn your window. For example thread some dried leaves carefully on to a strong thread, making sure that they are well spaced, so that the shapes can readily be seen. Of course you can also take leaves which are not yet dry, but they have the disadvantage of curling up and losing their colour in a heated room. If the leaves are well dried they will generally keep their colours (see page 64 for how to dry leaves).

Make a loop in the thread at both ends of the garland and fix it in place with pins on to the window-frame or tape it to the window itself.

If you are using corn grains take the fresh soft ones straight from the cob. If these are not available it is possible to take dried grains and boil them till they become soft.

Before threading bore a little hole in the beech-nut husks. Do the same for the acorns, acorn-cups and hazelnuts which have already

Figure 72.

been dried. If the pumpkin-seeds are still fresh and moist the needle will easily go right through them. But with dried seeds you must first bore a hole.

Of course it is not necessary to hang up all the garlands at the same time as is shown on Figure 73. Some of the fruits will slowly but surely shrivel up. So after a time an old garland can be replaced by a fresh one.

You can sometimes make a more attractive garland by not threading the fruits and nuts right up against each other and then thread lengths of straw in between.

Mobile with autumn garlands

All the fruits, chestnuts, nuts etc. on the garlands hanging down from this mobile are separated by little bits of straw of different lengths. To cut these straws, make a quick snip with a pair of very sharp scissors. If you cut too slowly, the scissors will flatten the straw and it may break.

As can be seen in Figure 73 many different things have been used for the garland, even little twig and corn silks. In this example a ring of plaited straw is used for the mobile other materials and forms are of course possible.

Figure 73.

7 Harvest Leaves

There are many things which can be made with dried leaves. It can become an absorbing activity to look for suitable autumn leaves. Medium-sized and smaller ones are most suitable. Collect leaves of many different shapes, for when arranging a pattern variety enhances the design.

Store dried leaves according to their kind, colour or size, in large envelopes. The leaves must however be thoroughly dry beforehand to prevent their becoming mouldy.

Working with fresh leaves

Materials
Fresh autumn leaves
Wallpaper or flour paste

Method
With autumn leaves you can of course make all sorts of things. Little children will nearly always want to do something right away with all the leaves which they have been collecting. Something which they can do is to stick the leaves on to the outside of a window with some paste. After a time the leaves will dry, many shrivel up and lose their colour, so with a little warm water all the bits can be washed off the window.

Drying leaves

The simplest way of drying autumn leaves is to lay them in an old telephone book, and leave them for about a week. Put some heavy books or bricks on top of the telephone book, to press the leaves flat. A flower-press or leaf-press is also useful.

Not all leaves lend themselves to being dried, for there are leaves, such as birch for example, which in the process of being dried lose their colour completely and become quite brown. Other leaves, such as chestnut are best picked off the tree while the inside of the leaf is still green and a little yellow-brownish edge appears round it (see the illustration on the title page).

A leaf and flower press

Materials

Two plywood boards 8″ × 8″ (20 × 20 cm) and ³/₈″ (8 mm) thick

6–8 pieces of corrugated cardboard 8 × 8″ (20 × 20 cm)

A number of sheets of tissue-paper 8 × 8″ (20 × 20 cm)

4 bolts, 2″ (4–6 cm) long, ¼″ (6 mm) diameter (No 14), with wing-nuts and washers

Method

Sandpaper the plywood boards. Draw the two diagonals to find the right place to make the holes, which should be about 1″ (2–3 cm) from the corners. Press the bolts through the holes of one of the boards, hammering them in tight if necessary. Cut off the corners of the corrugated cardboard and the tissue-papers so that they fit inside the bolts of the boards. Lay a few sheets of tissue-paper between each layer of cardboard. Finally lay the other board on top, fit the washers and tighten the nuts.

You can decorate the wooden boards of the flower-press with crayon or water-colours.

To dry and press flowers and leaves to be stored, lay them between two sheets of tissue-paper to ensure that any special features are preserved. If any parts of the flower should be too thick, such as a root, a stalk, a twig or the beginning of the fruit, carefully cut away the parts which are too thick with a sharp knife (or razor-blade), or even cut the stalk in half. The flowers should be kept in the press for a few weeks in order to dry out thoroughly.

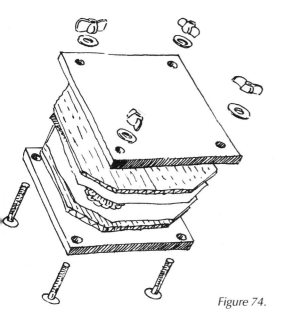

Figure 74.

A window decoration of dried leaves

Materials:
Autumn leaves
A large sheet of tracing paper
Modelling cement or glue

Method
Figure 75 shows an ornamental border of dried autumn leaves. It is not advisable to glue or cement the leaves directly on to the window because scraping them off again entails a lot of work (though paste can be washed off with warm water). It is also easier to make the border lying flat to try out the colour-layering and leaf combinations.

65

Figure 75.

Take a large sheet of tracing paper, cut to the size of the window. Lay out the decorations loose on to the paper so that you can see when the combination is right. Once the decoration is finished the borders of the tracing paper will be completely covered with leaves and no longer visible. Cut out the centre of the tracing paper (the border-frame can also be made with strips of paper joined together). The decoration shown in Figure 75 was made on a large sheet of tracing paper the middle of which was cut out leaving a border frame 4″ (10 cm) wide.

Begin by arranging on a table a number of leaves overlapping each other to make a corner. Keep rearranging the leaves until they give a pleasing appearance, but take care with them as dried leaves are brittle. Then stick the leaves one by one on to the tracing paper in the right place. Because the leaves have been dried it is best not to use a water-based paste. Modelling cement is the best: it sticks well and dries quickly. Remove surplus adhesive quickly.

After each item allow the glue to dry so that everything remains in place. Lay something heavy on top (such as a thick book). If you do not wish to wait while the first batch is drying, continue in another corner. While the glue is drying there you can go back to the first part.

When the border is finished it can be stuck to the inside of a window with some adhesive tape. After removing it the decoration can be stored between two sheets of card.

Transparencies

Materials
Dried leaves and grasses
Stout cardboard
Tracing paper
Modelling cement

Method
Cut out a frame from the cardboard. The form can be rectangular, circular or oval as desired.

Draw the outline of the frame again on the tracing paper. Select some good leaves and/or grasses. Stick these with as little glue as possible on to the tracing paper. Then stick the cardboard frame on to it and dry the whole thing under weight.

Figure 76.

Postcards and notepaper

Materials
Autumn leaves
Card
Sheets of notepaper
Plastic foil, sticky on one side

Method
Figure 77 shows some cards and notepaper simply decorated with leaves. Often only one beautifully shaped leaf is all that is necessary, but it is also possible to embellish a whole card making your own picture postcard.

Cement the dried leaves on to the paper or card and allow it to dry under weight. With a picture postcard it is better to cover the leaves with plastic foil.

Figure 77.

A crown of leaves

Materials
Large autumn leaves, for example, sycamore or maple

Method
You can easily see in Figure 78 how this crown of leaves is made. First cut off the stems and keep them. Lay one leaf partly over another and press a stem through them both to keep them together. Continue until the crown has reached the desired length. If necessary strengthen the crown by sticking a strip of sticky tape along the inside. Finally stick the two ends together and the crown is finished.

Figure 78.

8 Autumn, Michaelmas and Hallowe'en

As we mentioned in the Foreword there are two festivals in the autumn: September 29 is Michaelmas, the feast of Michael and his angels, and October 31 is Hallowe'en. Legends tell of the Archangel Michael overcoming the dragon.

Michael and the dragon from harvest leaves

Materials
Autumn leaves
Tracing paper
Figure 79.

Method
Making Michael and the dragon from dried leaves is similar to the window ornament on page 65. This time not only the border is decorated, but a whole picture is made.

Cut the tracing paper to fit the window frame. It is advisable first to sketch out on a piece of paper what you have in mind. Then begin at one corner of the paper to lay the leaves but this time without overlapping.

Make sure that when the parts are finished they can be dried under weight. As in Figure 79 you do not have to cover the whole sheet of paper, leave some parts open to allow light to shine through.

Decorating candles

Materials
A thick candle
(Bees) wax-foil in various colours
A thick darning-needle or palette-knife

Method
Candles can be decorated in several ways. In all cases the wax which we are going to use for the decoration should first be made soft and work-able. This can be done by taking a small amount of wax in your hand and working it with your fingers until it becomes soft. Stick the wax on to the candle and work it into the desired shape.

The decorating-wax must be properly warm when it is being stuck to the candle. Repeat this until the picture is complete.

You can also spread the wax very thinly on the candle, drawing it out as you stick it on. This gives a water-colour layering effect.

Figure 80.

Candlesticks made of clay

Materials
Modelling clay
A candle
Water-colours (if desired)

Method
Always shape the candlestick out of one piece of clay. Do not add on other bits, as they can break off once the clay has dried.

First make the candle-hole to fit a particular candle, but remove the candle from the hole while the clay is drying, because clay contracts while drying and with the candle in it, the clay can split. Once the clay has dried you might like to paint the candlestick.

Figure 80 shows two dragon-candlesticks. Children enjoy modelling these creatures.

Cobwebs

Materials
A fine big chestnut
Barbecue-skewers or cocktail-sticks
Coloured wool
Silver thread
An awl or large needle

Method
With the awl or large needle make at least seven holes round the chestnut. Then insert a cocktail stick or barbecue skewer into each hole. For a large cobweb use barbecue skewers, for a small cobweb cocktail-sticks.

Select a coloured wool, tie one end on to one of the sticks and press the wool hard against the chestnut. Lead the wool from stick to stick, and round each stick (Figure 81). Continue until a colour strip becomes quite evident. Cut the wool, and tie on another colour and continue. Make the knots as small as possible and see that they lie at the back of the web. The nice round side of the chestnut is of course the front. By changing the colours you get the effect shown in Figure 81. Finish off by tying the wool on to one of the sticks.

Variation 1:
The cobweb in Figure 82 is made according to the same principle, but only use one colour, and leave space between the rounds, so that a real web is made.

Figure 81.

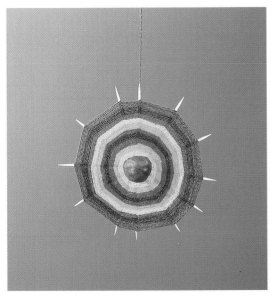

Figure 82.

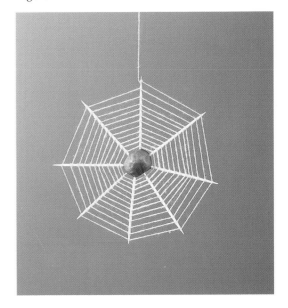

Variation 2:
For the cobweb in Figure 83 silver thread is used, giving the appearance of dew on the cobweb.

Instead of barbecue skewers use four thin branches to make a frame and drill two or three holes at regular intervals through each branch.

Now make a number of holes right through the chestnut. Thrust the needle and silver thread first through a hole in one of the twigs and then through the chestnut and then again through a hole in the twig of the frame on the other side (for example from top right to bottom left). Plug the thread temporarily into the frame with broken cocktail sticks.

Figure 83.

When all the threads have been attached provisionally to the chestnut, pull out the cocktail sticks one by one and pull the threads tight. Then thrust the sticks firmly into the twigs and cut off the protruding bit.

Now start weaving the web. When the cobweb is big enough tie the end with a little knot and cut off the surplus threads.

Finally you can make two holes to hang up the cobweb frame.

A dragon made of chestnut husks

Materials
Conker husks or horse-chestnut husks
Cocktail-sticks
Chestnut leaves
Red berries or rosehips

Method
Select a number of chestnut husks which are still closed. Use a husk which is a little open for the mouth. Attach the husks to each other with cocktail-sticks. Figure 84 shows what still has to be done to make the dragon look fierce. Of course this is only one way of making a dragon — imagination will allow many possibilities.

Figure 84.

A sling

Materials
A chestnut or a pine-cone
A strip of crêpe-paper 20″ × 6″ (50 × 15 cm)
A piece of string

Method
Cut the length of crêpe-paper into thin strips about ½″ (1 cm) leaving them joined together at one end. Roll the uncut end together and tie the string firmly to it. Now take the chestnut (or pine-cone), bore a hole through the middle and tie it to the other end of the string. Now the sling is finished and you can twirl it round hard and let it go. Watch that no one is in the way!

Figure 85.

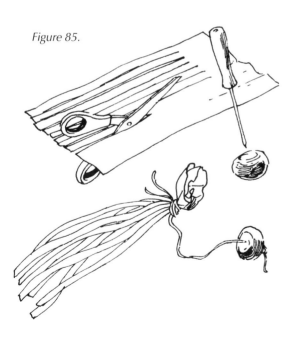

A kite

Materials
A long lath 32″ (80 cm) about ⅝″ (15 mm) in
    diameter
A cross lath 24″ (60 cm) about ⅝″ (15 mm) in
    diameter
A piece of wood 8″ (20 cm) long (to wind on the
    kite-line)
Coloured kite-paper
Strong thin string
Kite-line of about 300 feet (100 m)
Glue

Method
Notch both ends of the two laths and tie them tightly together with string to make a cross. Then tie a thin string from corner to corner and pull taut (Figure 87). Now the frame is finished.

Measure and mark the kite-paper to be cut out making sure that it overlaps the frame by about 2″ (5 cm) larger. Strengthen the corners by sticking on an extra bit of kite-paper. Lay the wooden cross on to the paper, fold the edges back over the taut string and stick down. Then lay the kite flat on the table and insert two strings at the four corners of the frame through the kite paper; one string joins the ends of the cross-lath, the other those of the long lath. Then tie the strings to the notched ends of the laths.

Tie both strings into a loop in the middle above the crossing point. When you now lift the kite (upside-down) by the string the tail-end of the kite will hang a bit lower than the head end.

The tail is four times as long as the kite itself. Tie knots at roughly 8″ (20 cm) intervals as in the sketch to take coloured strips of paper. Fix a brush of paper strips at the end of the tail. The kite-line and the tail are detachable for convenience in carrying and storing. Just before flying the kite attach them to the kite, each by a wooden toggle in a loop of line.

Finally tension the cross-lath below with a string to make a bow, which will make the kite more stable in the air. When you go to fly the kite take materials to repair the kite with you in case it becomes damaged after an accidental nose-dive.

Fly your kite in open spaces and *never* fly it near electricity lines.

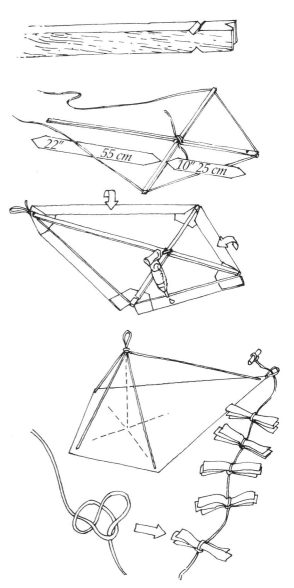

Figure 86.

Figure 87.

75

A dragon-loaf

Materials to make 1¾ lb (800 g) loaf
About 18 oz (500 g) white flour, fine wheatmeal
    or a mixture of both
10 fl oz (275 cc) lukewarm milk
½ tablespoon yeast
1¾ oz (50 g) hard butter
Just under ½ tablespoon salt
1 yolk of an egg (optional)

Method
Measure the flour into a mixing-bowl and make a hole in the middle (keep back a few spoonfuls for kneading). Dissolve the yeast into the milk, pour the mixture into the hole in the flour and stir it from the middle outwards bringing in the flour to make a runny rough.

Cut the butter into very thin strips and lay these on top of the dough. Sprinkle the salt on to the butter.

Leave this mixture to stand for a quarter of an hour until bubbles have formed. During fermentation some warmth is released and the butter is softened. Now you can lay the yolk over it. Stir it all with a fork from the middle outwards till it becomes a firm but tacky dough.

Now sprinkle the remains of the flour on to the kneading board, empty the dough scraping the dish, sprinkle some of the flour over the dough and knead it all to an elastic dough until it no longer sticks to the board or to your hands, using more flour if necessary. Do not knead for too long, otherwise the warmth of your hands will melt the butter and you will press it out and the dough will become sticky.

Now put the lump of dough back into the bowl. Put the bowl into a plastic bag or cover it with a damp cloth and allow the dough to rise

to twice its volume in room temperature (1–2 hours) or in the refrigerator (3 hours or overnight). Dough which has risen cold is more easily formed.

Now shape the dough into the form of a dragon, lay it on to a baking-tray and allow it once more to rise to twice its volume (loosely covered with clingfilm at room temperature). Paint the loaf with egg-yolk loosely stirred with the same amount of milk or water. Bake 10 minutes at 225°C, (450°F, gasmark 7–8) and then 15 minutes at 200°C (400°F, gasmark 6).

Figure 88.

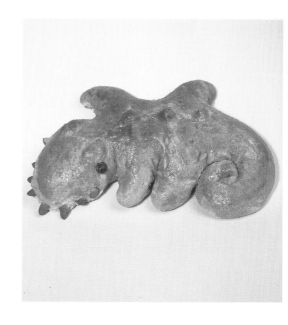

A transparency for the table

Materials
Thick cardboard coloured on one side
Coloured tissue-paper
A sheet of tracing paper

Method
This kind of transparency you can put any-where: on a table, on a box, or in front of the window. Light a candle behind it.

On the back of the cardboard draw the shape of the framework. The transparency in Figure 89 is a triptych. Cut out the outside shape, and with the back of a round knife score along the line where the sides are to be folded. In the transparency shown here the design is cut out of the cardboard from the edge and the colours of the tissue-paper only make the background.

If, for example, you have drawn a boy with a lantern on the back of the cardboard then you can cut out the cardboard round him. Then stick a piece of tracing paper behind all the open parts.

Tear out the shapes which you require for the background from the tissue-paper. Stick the pieces of tissue-paper on and so gradually build up the transparency by laying colour layer on to colour layer.

A transparency for the window

Materials
A large sheet of tracing paper
Tissue-paper in various colours
Starch (paste)

Figure 89.

Figure 90.

Method

The size of the transparency is determined by the window where it is to be hung. Apply these measurements to the sheet of tracing paper. Now stick it to the window with some adhesive tape. The transparency shown in Figure 90 is also made by tearing. If you find it difficult simply to tear out a shape freehand you can sketch the shape on a loose sheet of tracing paper and stick this sheet between the window and the paper.

You can see if you have the tissue-paper of a particular colour which you want, but it is much more fun to try to bring out the colour itself by laying several layers of different coloured paper over each other.

Tear out an odd piece from the tissue-paper and see how it fits into the form of the transparency. Continue in the same way with the next piece. Only with special things such as the sword will you have to think of the exact shape; for the rest this tearing method gives you a lot of freedom as the shapes do not have to be exact.

A Hallowe'en lantern

Materials
A turnip or pumpkin
A sharp knife
A spoon
An apple-corer
A night-light in a tin
Wire

Method
Cut a slab about 1"–2" (2–5 cm) thick from the top of the pumpkin or turnip. Hollow the turnip out by using a knife, spoon or apple-corer. This is best done by sticking the apple-corer into the turnip each time and then scooping out the loose bits with a spoon. Continue until the turnip is completely hollowed out. The walls of the turnip should remain about ¼"–½" (5–10 mm) thick. Make the bottom flat with a hole in the middle to take the night-light.

With a sharp knife carve out carefully sun, moon and stars in the outside of the turnip without cutting through the walls, these designs being peeled off.

With the apple-corer make three holes in the lid for air to allow the light to burn. Insert the wire left and right through the turnip and through the lid. Make the loops big enough so that the lid can be moved up and down for lighting the light.

Figure 91.

9 Tools and Materials

Finally I wish to say something here about tools and materials. In order to make many of the things described, a certain amount of basic equipment and materials will be necessary.

Tools

The following are useful and are not always mentioned in the text:
A pair of strong scissors for cutting all kinds of
    things
A pair of small pointed scissors
A pair of small pincers
A pair of small pointed pliers
A gimlet
An awl or bodkin
A sharp knife
A pair of tweezers
A few thick needles

Materials

It is good to start collecting materials for decorations during the summer. The materials used in this book can be found anywhere, even in cities. Where the plant or tree described here may not grow, there are others which can be used instead.

However, it may be difficult to find grain of suitable lengths. The revived interest in making decorations has resulted in a few shops stocking these.

Take care to dry everything well before storing, as this will prevent mould growing.

Paper and board

Tissue paper is thin, brightly coloured, semi-
    transparent paper.
Kite paper is thicker, shiny coloured,
    semitransparent paper.
Tracing paper is available in blocks as well as in
    rolls.
Crêpe paper is stretchable in a variety of bright
    colours.
Board is smooth, about 300 gsm or 3-ply.
Coloured board comes in gold, silver or other
    colours on one side.

Adhesives

Flour paste can be made up simply by mixing
    flour with a little water, and is suitable for
    paper.
Wallpaper glue comes as a powder to be mixed
    with water. Don't mix too much!
There are various *white water-soluble glues*
    (polymer medium) available under different
    names in different countries.
Glue sticks are useful as it is easier to get a thin

layer which will not buckle or stain thin paper.

Rubber cement (like Cow gum) is available in tubes or pots. It needs a thin layer pasted on each side of paper or board; leave to dry, and then press the surfaces firmly together. Excess cement can be rubbed away, forming a little spongy ball. The disadvantage is the toxic fumes, and it does yellow with age.

Household cement is a fast drying vinyl-based glue in a tube (like Uhu). It is very strong, but does have drawbacks: flammability, toxic fumes, and it often strings.

Candles and wax

Watch with *candles* not to get the cheapest which are made of loose particles, coated in a layer of wax. When pressed too hard they will crumble, spoiling any decoration.

Modelling wax and *decorating wax* are made by Stockmar. Stockmar products can be obtained in some shops. They are distributed in the United States by HearthSong, PO Box B, Sebastopol, CA 95473; in Britain obtainable from Helios Fountain, 7 Grassmarket, Edinburgh EH1 2HY; in New Zealand from Ceres Enterprises, PO Box 11-336, Auckland.

Other materials

Straws. Some craft shops may have packets of thick and thin straws for craft work. If they cannot be found there, they must be obtained from a farmer at harvesting time. Cut the straw to avoid nodes in the lengths to be used for making stars. If the straws are to be cut open, thick straws are needed.

Wire

The *copper wire* most commonly used here is 1/32" (0.8 mm) in diameter.

Florist's wire is very thin green or dark brown wire, available in craft shops or garden centres.